Five Famous Fairy Tales

Level 2

Retold by Jane Rollason
Series Editors: Andy Hopkins and Jocelyn Potter

Pearson Education Limited
Edinburgh Gate, Harlow,
Essex CM20 2JE, England
and Associated Companies throughout the world.

ISBN 0 582 42125 X

This edition first published 2000

NEW EDITION

Copyright © Penguin Books Ltd 2000
Illustrations by Gwen Tourret
Cover design by Bender Richardson White

Typeset by Pantek Arts Ltd, Maidstone, Kent
Set in 11/14pt Bembo
Printed in Denmark by Nørhaven A/S, Viborg

Published by Pearson Education Limited in association with
Penguin Books Ltd, both companies being subsidiaries of Pearson Plc

For a complete list of the titles available in the Penguin Readers series
please write to your local Pearson Education office or to: Marketing Department,
Penguin Longman Publishing, 5 Bentinck Street, London, W1M 5RN.

Contents

Introduction

Jacob and Wilhelm Grimm – the Brothers Grimm – were good friends. Jacob was a quiet man and sometimes sad. Wilhelm was often very ill but he was a happier person than his brother. He had a wife and children.

The brothers' stories came from friends and family. They paid one poor old man for his story with some new trousers. A woman from the next village sold them eggs and told them stories. Their first book came out in Germany in 1812, when Jacob and Wilhelm were nearly forty.

Hans Andersen came from Denmark and wrote more than 150 fairy tales. He was the son of a poor shoemaker, and his mother couldn't read. But his father read him the *Arabian Nights* and the young Hans began to love stories. At the age of 14 he went to Copenhagen and got some work in the theatre. A very kind man helped him at university, and at the age of 23 he was a writer. In 1835 his first book of fairy tales came out. 'The Glass Box' was one of these stories. He wrote for people of all ages.

Another name for the *Arabian Nights* is the *Thousand and One Nights*. Aladdin, Ali Baba, Sindbad and a story in this book, 'The Fisherman and the Giant', are all from the *Thousand and One Nights*. There was a king in Arabia, and his wife loved another man. The king killed her and now he hated women. He married a new woman every day and killed her the next morning. But then he married Sheherezade. She told him a story every night but she didn't tell him the end. So the king had to wait for the next evening and he could not kill her. After a thousand and one nights, Sheherezade had no more stories. But now the king loved her and did not want to kill her.

The Table, the Donkey and the Stick

Once there was a woman with three sons – Tom, Bob and Jack. Tom was the youngest. Bob came next, and Jack was the oldest. They lived in a village. They were happy, but their mother was very poor. So the boys looked for work.

◆

Tom worked for a kind man in the next town. The man made tables and other things from wood. Tom worked very hard for one year. When the year ended, the kind man gave him a table. It looked old and dirty, but it was a magic table.

'Say to the table, "I am hungry." Then wonderful food will appear on it by magic,' said the man, with a smile.

'You are very kind,' said Tom to the man. And he left. He went from country to country and from city to city, and he was always happy. He carried his table on his back. When he wanted food, he put the table down – in the street, by a river, under a tree. He said to the table, 'I am hungry', and lovely food appeared.

Some months later, he thought, 'I would like to see my mother. I'll go home.'

On the last night of his journey to his mother's house, he came to an old house. An old man lived there.

'Can I stay the night here?' he asked the old man.

'Yes, you can stay here, but I can't give you any food,' said the old man.

'Don't give me any food,' Tom said. '*You* can eat with *me*.' Then he put down his table and said, 'I am hungry.' Wonderful food appeared and they ate it.

Now this man was not a good man. He was a jealous man.

'I want this boy's table,' he thought. 'It will give me food. I can sell the food to other people. I will never be hungry again.'

He said to the table, 'I am hungry', and lovely food appeared.

When Tom was asleep that night, the old man took the magic table from Tom's room. He worked all night and made a new table. It looked the same. He put it next to Tom's bed.

The next morning Tom put the new table on his back and he walked to his mother's house.

Tom's mother was very happy when she saw her youngest son. 'What did you do when you were away?' she asked.

'I made tables,' said Tom. 'And I have a table here.'

'It's not a very nice table,' said his mother.

'But it's a *magic* table,' answered Tom. 'When I say to it, "I am hungry", beautiful food appears on it.'

'Show me!' said his mother.

'Let's invite our friends from the village. Then everybody can see the magic,' said Tom.

Tom's mother invited everybody from the village. Tom put his table down in front of them and said, 'I am hungry.' But nothing happened. No wonderful food appeared on the table. Everybody laughed and went away. Tom was very angry. He knew now – the old man had his magic table.

Tom was very unhappy. He ran away from home and went back to his old job. He wrote to his brother, Jack. His letter told the story of the magic table and the jealous old man.

◆

Bob, the second brother, worked with a friendly man in a village many kilometres away. Bob worked very hard for one year. When the year ended, the man gave Bob a donkey.

'You can't sit on this donkey,' the man said, 'but it is a good donkey.'

'It's very small. Why is it a good donkey?' asked Bob.

'Because it's a magic donkey,' answered the man. 'Put a box under its mouth. Say the magic word, "Bricklebat", and gold will suddenly fall from its mouth. Catch the gold in the box. You will never be poor.'

'You are very kind,' Bob said to the man. Bob went from country to country, and from city to city, and he was always happy. He took the donkey with him. He bought the most expensive clothes and ate the most wonderful food. He stayed in the best houses. When he wanted more money, he said 'Bricklebat' to the donkey.

Some months later, Bob thought, 'I would like to see my mother. I'll go home.'

On the last night of his journey, he came to the old house. The jealous old man was there.

'Can I stay the night here?' he asked.

'Yes, you can stay here, but I want money for your food and your bed.'

'Money!' cried Bob. 'You can have a lot of money!'

Bob ate lovely food at Tom's table. The old man asked for some money. Bob put his hand in his coat but there was nothing in it.

'Wait,' said Bob, 'I'll get some.'

He took a box and went outside to the donkey. The old man followed him to the door. He stood behind the door and Bob did not see him.

'Where is his money?' the old man thought. 'I'll watch him. When he's asleep, I'll take his money.'

Bob put the box under the donkey's mouth. He said the magic word. The gold fell into the box. The old man's mouth opened wider and wider.

'I want that donkey,' he thought.

Later that night, when Bob was asleep, the old man went outside. He found another donkey and put it in the place of the magic donkey.

The next morning, Bob took the new donkey and walked to his mother's house.

Bob's mother was very happy when she saw her son.

'What did you do when you were away?' she asked.

'I worked for a man,' said Bob. 'And he gave me this donkey.'

'It's a very small donkey,' said his mother. 'Is it strong?'

'No,' answered Bob, 'but it's a *magic* donkey. When I say the magic word, gold falls from its mouth. Call your friends. Let's show them.'

Everybody came from the village.

'Now, watch this!' said Bob. 'Bricklebat!' Everybody looked at the donkey. The donkey looked at them. Nothing happened. No gold fell from its mouth. Everybody laughed, and Bob was very angry. He knew now – the old man had his magic donkey. He ran away from home and went back to his old job. He wrote to his brother, Jack. His letter told the story of the magic donkey and the jealous old man.

◆

Jack worked with a wood-cutter. He worked very hard for one year. When the year ended, the wood-cutter gave Jack a beautiful box. There was a stick inside it.

'Thank you for the beautiful box,' said Jack, 'but I don't want the stick. I'll put something prettier than a stick in this lovely box.'

'It's a magic stick,' said the wood-cutter. 'When somebody is unkind to you, the stick will help you. You say, "Stick! Out of the box!" The stick will jump out of the box and it will hit them. When you say, "Stick! Back in the box!", it will stop hitting them.'

Jack took the box and started his journey home. On the last night of his journey, he came to the old house. The jealous old man was there. He gave Jack some food. Then Jack told him about his journey.

'Do you know,' said Jack, 'that there is a magic table? You say "I am hungry" to the table. Then wonderful food appears on it. And there is a magic donkey. You say "Bricklebat!" to it, and gold falls from its mouth. But I have something better than the magic table or the magic donkey in this box. Nothing in the world is as good as this!'

5

'What is it?' thought the jealous old man. 'I want it.'

When Jack went to bed, he put the box on the floor. He shut his eyes. After some time, the old man came into Jack's room. He looked at Jack. Quietly he put his hand on the box. Suddenly, Jack jumped out of bed. 'Stick! Out of the box!' he cried. The stick hit the jealous old man on his head and arms and back. The old man wanted to run away but he couldn't.

'Give me the magic table and the magic donkey. Then I will put the stick back in the box,' said Jack.

'Yes, yes,' cried the old man. 'You can have them. Stop the stick! Stop the stick!'

The next day, Jack took the table, the donkey and the stick and he walked to his mother's house.

Jack's mother was very happy when she saw her son.

'What did you do when you were away?' she asked.

'I worked with a wood-cutter,' said Jack. 'He gave me this stick.'

'A stick!' cried his mother angrily. 'Why did he give you a stick? You can get a stick from every tree in the world!'

'Yes,' said Jack. 'But this is a *magic* stick. When somebody is unkind to me, I say, "Stick! Out of the box!" It jumps out of the box and hits them. It only stops when I say, "Stick! Back in the box!" My brothers had a magic table and a magic donkey. A jealous old man took them. With this stick, I got them back again.'

◆

Jack's mother was very happy. She wrote to Tom and Bob and told them the story. They came home. She invited everybody from the village to their house. Everybody sat round the magic table and ate wonderful food. Everybody took home a bag of gold from the magic donkey's mouth.

From that day, the old woman and her three sons lived very happily.

The Prince and the Servants

Once there was a bad and jealous queen. She had a kind and beautiful daughter. Many princes from many countries wanted to marry the princess. The queen said to each prince, 'Before you marry my daughter, you have to do something for me.' And then she gave him an impossible job. When he couldn't do it, she said, 'Now you will die.' And her wood-cutter cut off his head.

'You will never marry,' she said to her unhappy daughter. And she laughed.

◆

Prince Charles was the son of a poor king in a small country. He heard about the beautiful princess. He said to his father, 'I want to marry her.'

'Never!' cried the king. 'The queen will kill you. You are my only son – I cannot lose you! There are hundreds of beautiful women in the world. You don't have to marry this one.' But the prince was very sad. He couldn't eat. He couldn't sleep. In the end his father said, 'Go, then – go to the princess! I hope you will do better than the other princes. I hope I will see you again.'

The prince was very excited and he danced round his rooms. He ate a lot of food and got strong again. Then he began his journey. He had no servants because his father was poor. 'I'll find servants on the way,' he said.

After a short time, the prince saw a small mountain. 'What is that mountain?' he thought. 'It wasn't there before.'

He went nearer. It wasn't a mountain. It was a very fat man on his back, asleep. The prince went near him and the fat man woke up.

'What are you doing here, Fat Man?' asked the prince.

'I was asleep,' said Fat Man, 'and now I am not asleep. Because of you.'

'Why were you asleep?'

'Because I had some food this morning. Now I want my lunch.'

'What did you eat this morning?' asked the prince.

'Ten chickens and a hundred cakes,' said Fat Man.

'Will you be my servant?' asked the prince.

'Give me food,' said the Fat Man, 'and I will do anything for you.'

So the Fat Man followed the prince.

A short time later on their journey, they found another man. His head was down and his left ear was on the ground. He looked up. His left ear was very large.

'What are you doing, Big Ear?' asked the prince.

'I am listening,' said Big Ear. 'The flowers are opening. The birds are singing in a country over the sea. I can hear them.'

'What can you hear in the house of the beautiful princess?' asked the prince.

'People are crying. Another prince is dead.'

'Will you be my servant, Big Ear?'

'Yes,' said Big Ear, 'I will.'

A short time after that, they saw two long things by the road.

'What are they? Trees?' said Fat Man. They went nearer.

'They're not trees,' said Big Ear. 'They're arms. The longest arms in the world.' A little later they saw the man's head.

'You are a very long person,' said the prince.

'I can be longer than this,' said Long Arms.

'Come with me, Long Arms,' said the prince. 'Be my servant.'

So Long Arms followed the prince.

Next they saw a man with a hand over one eye.

'Is there something in your eye?' asked the prince.

'No,' said the man. 'I can see a long way. I can see through things – buildings, mountains, water. When something is near me, I have to put my hand over one eye. Then I can see it.'

'Come with me, Quick Eyes,' said the prince, 'and be my servant.' And Quick Eyes followed the prince.

They went on their journey and the sun got very hot. The prince opened his coat. They came to a man by the road. He wore two thick coats and a large hat. They could not see his face. He said, 'I am cold, cold, cold.'

'Why are you cold, Cold Man?' asked the prince. 'The sun is very hot and our coats and shirts are open. We are hot.'

'When I open my coat,' answered Cold Man, 'the sun disappears. It snows. Everything dies of cold.'

'Come with me,' said the prince, 'and be my servant. But please don't open your coat.' Cold Man went with the prince.

◆

Prince Charles and his servants arrived at the city, and the prince went to the queen.

'I want to marry the princess,' he said. 'What do I have to do?'

The queen answered, 'You will have to do three things. Do them well. Then you can marry the princess.'

'What is the first thing?' asked the prince.

'I have a beautiful blue jewel. Yesterday it fell into the river. Bring me the jewel before the sun goes down!'

The prince went back to his servants.

'How can we find the jewel?' he asked them.

Quick Eyes took his hand from his eye.

'I will look for it.' He went to the river. 'There it is – over there.'

'I can't see it,' said Long Arms.

Then Fat Man opened his mouth and drank the water in the river. A short time later, the river was dry. Long Arms got the jewel and gave it to the prince.

The queen was very angry when she saw the jewel. Then she said, 'Tomorrow I will give this prince a very difficult job.' She thought hard. She did not sleep that night.

The next morning the prince woke up early. He went to the queen again.

'You are hungry after your long journey,' she said, with a cold smile. 'I have thirty chickens outside. Eat them before twelve o'clock. I do not want to find *one* chicken leg.'

'Can I invite a friend?' the prince asked. 'I do not like eating without a friend.'

'You can ask one friend,' said the queen. The prince left. 'He will die this afternoon,' she said to her daughter. And she laughed.

The prince went back to his friends.

'Come with me, Fat Man,' he said.

Fat Man quickly ate the thirty chickens. Then he ate the queen's other animals, the bread in the kitchens, the fruit on the trees and the vegetables in the ground.

'*Now* what can I eat?' asked Fat Man. There was nothing there so he went to sleep.

At twelve o'clock the queen called for her lunch. She waited and waited, but no food came. She went to see the cook. 'Where is my lunch?' she asked.

'A fat man ate everything in the gardens and everything in the kitchens. There is no food.'

The queen got angrier and angrier. Then she thought of a plan. 'Ha ha!' she laughed. 'Now I will catch him.'

The prince came to her on the third day.

'Will you eat with me tonight?' she asked, with a lovely smile. 'And after that, would you like to sit with the princess for two hours?'

'Yes,' answered the prince. 'I would love that.'

'You will not fall asleep when you are talking to the princess?' asked the queen.

'Fall asleep!' cried the prince. 'Never!'

'When a person falls asleep with the princess,' said the queen, 'the princess disappears by magic. Then that person dies.'

The prince put on his most beautiful clothes. He ate with the queen. Their conversation was very cold. Servants brought wonderful food and wonderful drinks. When the prince turned away for a minute, the queen quickly put something into his glass of wine. The prince did not see. He drank the wine.

Then the queen took him to the princess. They climbed up many stairs to a high room. The princess sat sadly by the window. The red light of the evening sun lit up her beautiful face. The river below, the flowers round the window and her dress were the same colour.

The prince sat near the princess. They were very happy for a short time. But the prince's eyes suddenly felt heavy. He started to fall asleep. He couldn't hear the princess's words. His eyes shut. He was asleep.

Half an hour later, he opened his eyes again. The princess wasn't there! He looked everywhere in the room, but he couldn't find her! He ran to the window and looked out. He saw Big Ear below. He called to him, 'The princess isn't here. We have to find her in the next hour.' Long Arms brought the prince down to the ground.

'Where is the princess? Can you hear her, Big Ear?'

Big Ear put his ear to the ground.

'Yes,' he said. 'I can hear her. She is calling. She says that she is across the river. She is inside a tree. Her mother's men put her there.'

Quick Eyes looked. 'Yes,' he said, 'I can see her.'

'But how can we get her?' cried the prince. 'I have an idea,' said Cold Man and he opened his coat. Snow fell. Everything went white. Cold Man jumped into the river and the water was ice. They ran across the ice and brought the princess back. Long Arms put the prince and princess back through the window into the high room. They sat down and the door opened. The queen came in. She could not speak when she saw the princess. She gave them a cold smile.

The red light of the evening sun lit up her beautiful face.

'We are having a very interesting conversation,' said the prince. 'We are talking about trees and rivers.'

'Come with me,' said the queen. 'It is night. Your bedroom is ready. Your servants can sleep there too.'

The prince said goodnight to the princess and he and his servants followed the queen. She took them to a big room. The queen shut the door. She ran to the cook and said, 'Make a great fire under their room.'

After a short time the room got very hot. The prince went to the door but he couldn't open it.

'I can hear a great fire below us,' said Big Ear.

'This is wonderful,' said Cold Man. 'I feel really warm for the first time in my life.'

'Open your coat, Cold Man,' said the prince. When Cold Man opened his coat, the room got colder again. 'That's better,' they said.

The queen listened at the door. She heard them. She ran to the cook and said, 'Make the fire hotter.'

Cold Man smiled. 'I am warm again,' he said.

'They are cooking us,' said the other servants.

'Take off your coat,' said the prince. The prince took Cold Man's coat away.

'I am too cold,' said Cold Man. 'Please give me back my coat.'

Snow fell in the room. The prince could not speak because he was too cold. Fat Man cried. There was ice in his hair.

The queen came to the door. She listened. Nothing.

'They are dead now,' she said. She opened the door. The prince and his servants ran out of the room.

'Let's go and sit by a fire,' said the prince. 'My face and hands are blue with cold.'

The queen could not win – she knew that now. So she left the country. The princess married the prince and they lived happily. And the good servants lived with them.

The Glass Box

Once there was a poor man. His name was Hans. He had no money, no house and no food, but he was happy. 'I'll find something,' he said. 'I'll walk down this road to the next town.'

After a short time, a very old woman called to him from across the road.

'What do you want?' asked Hans.

'What do *you* want?' said the old woman.

'What do *I* want? I want money.'

'You can have money,' said the old woman. 'Take this magic blue coat and climb to the top of that tall tree. Then climb down inside it. You will come into a large room with three hundred lights. There are three doors. Go through the first door and you will see a big box. On the box sits a dog with eyes as large as eggs. Don't be afraid – it won't hurt you. Put my blue coat on the floor. Take the dog and put it down on the coat in front of the box. Open the box and you will see money. Take some.

'Go through the second door and you will see a bigger box. On the box sits a dog with eyes as large as oranges. Don't be afraid – it won't hurt you. Put the dog down on the coat in front of the box. Open the box and you will see gold. Take some.

'Go through the third door. There you will see the biggest box. On the box sits a dog with eyes as large as plates. Don't be afraid – it is friendly. There are jewels in its box. Take some.'

'This is wonderful,' said Hans. 'But what can *I* do for *you*?'

'I don't want any money or gold or jewels,' said the old woman. 'I only want one little thing. In the third room, there is a small glass box. My grandmother lost it there. Bring me that box.'

Hans climbed up the tree and then down inside the tree. He went down and down and down. Then he saw the three hundred lights and the three doors. He opened the first door and went into a little room. There, on a box, was a dog with eyes as large as eggs.

'Good dog!' said Hans. He remembered the old woman's words. He put her blue coat on the floor. He took the dog and put it down on the coat in front of the box. He opened the box and he got very excited. He took some money and put it in his hat. He put the dog back on the box and went into the second room.

There, on a box, was a dog with eyes as large as oranges.

'You're a fine dog!' said Hans. He put the dog down in front of the box, and opened the box. His eyes were suddenly as yellow as the gold in the box. Hans took some gold and put it in his hat.

Then he went into the last room. This dog's eyes were as large as plates. 'You are a very fine dog!' he said. Hans looked at the jewels in the box. His eyes were suddenly red, blue, yellow, green and gold. He took some jewels and put them in his shoes. Then he remembered the old woman's glass box. He found it on the floor next to the dog.

He climbed up inside the tree again. It was harder this time with the heavy gold and jewels, but he got out of the tree.

'Throw down the box,' called the old woman when she saw him. But he did not throw it. Suddenly a stone hit him on the head.

'Help! I'm going to fall and die,' he thought. But he put out a hand and he did not fall.

'Did you throw that stone?' he called.

'Yes. Now give me the box.' She was not very friendly now.

'I'm not going to give it to you,' he answered.

The old woman got very angry and her face was very ugly. He climbed to the ground and walked away down the road. She called him names but he did not answer. She could do nothing.

◆

It was night when he came to the town. He found a very nice room and asked for the best food. The next day he went out and bought beautiful clothes. He was a very important and rich man, people thought. He suddenly had many friends.

Hans took some gold and put it in his hat.

One day somebody asked him, 'Do you know about the princess?'

'What princess?' asked Hans. 'Who is she? Where does she live?'

'You cannot see her,' answered the man.

'Why not?'

'Because she is in a big house and she can't leave it. There is only one door. The windows are high up. She never goes out. The king says nobody can see her.'

'Why does she live in that way?' asked Hans.

'Because a clever old man said to the king, "Your daughter will marry a poor man." The king was very angry. He built the big house with high windows and shut the princess in it.'

'I want to see the princess,' said Hans. He found the house and went to the door. But the king's servants quickly sent him away. Then he put on his most expensive clothes and went to the king's home. The king was very angry. 'Don't come near my house again,' he shouted. 'I will cut off your head and put it on a stick.'

◆

Hans lived well at this time and quickly used his money. One day he only had two jewels. He left his nice room. He found a poor house and lived in it. Hans was poor now. Nobody cooked his food. Nobody cleaned his shoes. His rich 'friends' did not invite him to their homes. He tried to find the tree with the three dogs again, but he couldn't find it.

After a short time Hans had no money. No money for food. He looked round his room. What could he sell? There, on the table, he saw the little glass box.

'Perhaps I can buy some bread with this,' he thought. 'Why did the old woman want it? It is glass but I can't see into it. Perhaps there are jewels or gold inside.' He tried to open the box but he couldn't. He hit it once with his hand. Suddenly the dog with eyes as large as eggs appeared in front of him.

17

'What do you want?' asked the dog.

'What do I want!' cried Hans. 'I want money!'

The dog went away. It quickly came back with a bag of money in its mouth.

Hans thought. Then he said, 'I know! The first dog comes when I hit the box once. The second dog will come when I hit the box again. The third dog will come when I hit the box three times.'

He hit the box – one, two – and the dog with eyes as large as oranges brought gold. He hit the box three times – one, two, three – and the dog with eyes as large as plates brought jewels.

Hans was rich again. He bought beautiful clothes and moved to a big house. All his 'friends' came back.

'Why didn't you visit us?' they said. 'Where were you?'

Hans did not like these friends. He thought only of the sad princess.

'She can never go out,' he thought. 'She can never walk in the garden. Her mother is dead. She can only speak to the servants and the old king. She has an unhappy life.'

One night Hans could not sleep. Suddenly he had an idea and he got up from his bed. He took the glass box and hit it once. The dog came.

'It is night – a beautiful night,' said Hans, 'and nobody will see. I know that the princess would like a walk in my garden. Bring her here.'

Very quickly the dog came back. The princess was asleep on its back. Her beautiful face was sad.

Hans woke her and took her into the garden.

'Where am I?' she cried. 'What is happening?' She was afraid.

'You are walking with me in my garden,' said Hans. 'Look – the flowers are asleep.'

'A garden!' cried the princess. 'Am I outside? With the ground under my feet and the sky over my head? No walls? No windows? I can hear the sounds of the night round me!'

They walked for a long time. Then the sun started to appear. 'I have to go,' she said. 'But how did I get here?' Hans told her about the glass box and the dogs. She hit the box and called the dog.

'Good dog!' she said, when it appeared. 'You have beautiful eyes. Take me home. I don't want anybody to see us. Thank you for this night, Hans.' The princess climbed on the dog's back and fell asleep.

The next day the princess did not remember anything but she felt different. Her servant, Anna, a jealous and unkind woman, woke her. She said, 'Wake up, princess, it is the middle of the day. The king is waiting for you.'

'Is he?' said the princess and she jumped happily out of bed. 'Look, Anna, it's a beautiful day.'

Anna started to think. A number of things were strange. First, the princess always got up at seven o'clock, but today it was twelve o'clock. Second, the princess was always sad, but today, she was happy. Third, the bottom of the princess's nightdress was dirty. Fourth, there was a beautiful white flower on the princess's bedroom floor, but there were no white flowers in the king's garden.

Anna went to the king.

'Let's wait and watch,' said the king. 'When she goes out again, we'll follow her.'

Hans was in love with the princess. He thought about her all day and all night. After three days, he couldn't wait. He hit the glass box – one, two – and the dog with eyes as large as oranges appeared.

'Please bring the princess to my garden,' he said.

The dog went to the princess. But Anna was there, too. The dog carried the princess away on its back and Anna followed. The dog stopped at the door of a big house and went in. Anna wrote the letter 'X' on the door and went home.

Hans and the princess walked in the garden. Hans told the story of the old woman and the tree and the three dogs and the glass box. He told the princess about his poor mother and about his three brothers and three sisters. The princess loved his stories. She talked about her parents.

'My father was a great man and a good king,' she said. 'But when my mother died, he changed. Suddenly he was old and tired and sad. He shut me in that house. Now he gets angry about little things. He doesn't want to be king. He wants white flowers in his garden. My mother loved white flowers. But now his flowers always die.'

The red of the morning sun started to light up the sky. The princess said goodnight to Hans. He hit the box – one, two – and the second dog appeared. With its eyes as big as oranges, this dog could see everything. It saw the 'X' on the door and it told Hans.

'Ho ho!' laughed Hans. 'Come with me quickly and we will write "X"s on every door in this street, and the next ten streets!'

The next day, Anna told the king the story of the night. The king took Anna and some men to Hans's street.

'Here is the house,' cried Anna.

'No, here it is,' cried the king.

One of the men ran to them. 'The house is in the next street,' he said. 'There is an "X" on the door.' Every house had an "X" on its door. The king was very angry and went home.

Later that day, Anna thought of another plan. She went into her room and shut the door. She made a small bag and she put little white stones in the bag. She made a small cut in the bottom of the bag and then put it in the princess's clothes. 'Now,' she said, 'when the princess goes out, the little stones will fall onto the road. We can follow the stones to the house.'

That night Hans called the princess again with the glass box. They walked in the garden. The dog with eyes as large as plates waited at the front of the house.

'I would like to be a prince,' said Hans.

'I would like *not* to be a princess,' said the princess.

'Why?' asked Hans. She didn't answer. 'I want to be a prince,' he said, 'because I want to marry you.' They sat down under a tree. Hans put the glass box on the ground next to him.

'Don't be a prince,' she said. 'I can't love a prince. I will be a poor girl and you will be Hans.'

At that minute the dog saw the king and Anna with a hundred servants. They came out of the king's house and looked at the little white stones. The white stones shone in the dark and they followed them. The dog ran to the princess.

'The king! The king is coming!' it cried. 'Come quickly!' The dog ran away through the streets with the princess on its back.

The king, Anna and the servants arrived at Hans's house. 'Is the princess here?' cried the king. Hans didn't answer. Suddenly the king saw his daughter's little shoe on the ground next to some beautiful white flowers. He couldn't speak for a minute. Then he said angrily to Hans, 'My wood-cutter will cut off your head at twelve o'clock tomorrow.' The servants took Hans to the king's house and shut him in a room.

Hans looked for his glass box. Where was it? Lost! He could not call the dogs. Then he remembered. It was under the tree.

When the sun came up, Hans went to the window and looked out. He was very high up. He saw a little boy below him and called to him.

'Hey! Little boy!'

'What do you want?' cried the boy.

'Would you like threepence?'

'Yes, please,' said the boy.

'Then run to my house. Say to my servant, "Hans has a little glass box. It is in the garden under a tree. He wants me to bring it to the king's house." When you bring me the box, I will give you threepence.'

The boy disappeared. A little time later he came back with the box.

'Throw it up to me,' called Hans. The boy threw up the box and Hans caught it. Then he threw down the money.

At that minute, the door opened and the king's men came in. They took Hans to a big square in the centre of the town. Everybody from the town was there. They wanted to watch. The king stood in the middle of the square with the important people of the town round him. In front of Hans stood a big strong wood-cutter. He wore a long red coat and a tall black hat.

'Are you ready?' said the king to the wood-cutter.

'Are you ready?' said the wood-cutter to Hans.

'No!' cried Hans, and he took out the glass box.

'Are you ready?' said the wood-cutter to Hans.

'No!' cried Hans, and he hit the box once. He hit the box again – one, two – and then again – one, two, three. The three dogs stood in front of him.

'Take the wood-cutter away,' he said to the dog with eyes as large as eggs. 'Throw him in the river.' The dog ran away with the wood-cutter on his back.

'Take the king's men away,' Hans said to the dog with eyes as large as plates. The dog got bigger and bigger. Everybody watched with open mouths. Now the dog was as big as a house. The king's men were very afraid and ran away.

'Bring the princess here,' Hans said to the dog with eyes as big as oranges. 'Where is the king?' he cried.

In a short time the princess and the king stood in front of Hans with the dogs behind them.

'Do you want to be king?' Hans asked the old king.

'No,' said the king. 'I only want to have white flowers in my garden, and a happy daughter.'

'When the princess and I marry, white flowers will live in your garden again and the princess will be happy.'

◆

And so Hans married the princess. The new king and queen lived happily for many years. They had six children and a very big garden. The old king lived his last years near them. His garden was a sea of white flowers all year.

The Fisherman and the Giant

Once there was a poor fisherman. He never caught many fish and so he had no money. On some days he did not catch any fish. He couldn't buy food for his wife and three children. They only ate fish!

Usually he caught very small fish, but one day he caught a dead horse. 'Today is a bad day,' he thought.

Angrily, he began to fish again. This time he caught a bag of old cups. Sadly, he threw them back in the water. 'What can I do?' he said. 'I am a poor man. I want to sell fish. I want to buy food for my children.'

He tried again. This time he caught an old jar. It looked green, but then he looked again. It was dirty. So he washed it and it was gold. There were some words on the top of the jar, but he couldn't read.

The fisherman jumped up happily. 'I can sell this now,' he said. 'Today is a good day.'

He looked at the jar carefully. 'Perhaps there is something inside,' he thought. 'I'll open it.' So he opened the jar and looked inside. Suddenly white smoke came out of the jar and a great giant appeared. The fisherman was very afraid. The giant spoke. 'Now, fisherman. I am going to kill you.'

'Why?' cried the fisherman. 'What did I do?'

'You opened the jar. For that I am going to kill you. How do you want to die? I can kill you with my hands, or I can throw you into the sea.'

Suddenly white smoke came out of the jar and a great giant appeared.

'But *why* do you have to kill me?'

'I will tell you,' said the giant.'One day, the King of the Giants was very angry with me. I took his youngest and loveliest daughter for a walk by the sea and he didn't like it. So he put me in this jar. I could not get out because he wrote his name on the top of the jar. I could hear him from inside the jar."Because you love the sea, you dog," he cried, "you can live in it!" And he threw me in the water.

'I was in the jar for days and weeks."One day somebody will open this bottle," I thought. "And I will make them into a great king or queen." But after a hundred years, nobody opened the bottle. So I thought, "I will make them into a king or queen but not a great king or queen." After 200 years, I thought, "Where is this person? Now I will make them rich, but I will not make them a king or queen." After 300 years, I was very angry. "When somebody opens the jar, I will kill them," I thought. You are that person, Fisherman. How do you want to die?'

'I have one question,' said the fisherman.'Will you answer it?'

'I will,' said the giant,'but ask quickly.'

'Were you in that jar?'

'Yes, I was,' answered the giant.'You saw me.'

'But you are so big.Your hand is as big as the jar. Think before you speak. Is there nothing inside your head?'

The giant was not very clever. 'I will show you,' he said angrily. Suddenly he disappeared into white smoke again, and the smoke went inside the jar. 'You see!' he called from inside. The fisherman quickly put the top back on the jar.

'Hah! Now, Giant,' he said.'I will throw the jar back into the sea. Perhaps somebody will find you in another 300 years.'

'Please open the jar,' called the Giant. 'I will make you a rich man.'

'No.You will kill me,' answered the fisherman.

'No, I won't,' said the giant. 'I won't. I'll make you very, very rich.'

The fisherman thought for a minute. 'All right, then,' he said, and opened the jar. White smoke came out of the jar and the giant appeared again. He quickly threw the jar into the sea.

'Thank you,' he said to the fisherman. 'I will not forget this. Come with me.' The fisherman followed the giant round the city walls and over a mountain. There they came to a great blue and gold sea. In the water there were many fish.

'Now, catch something. I will watch you,' said the giant. In no time, the fisherman caught three fish – three beautiful red, white and gold fish. 'Take these fish to your king,' said the giant. 'He will give you a lot of money for them.'

The giant disappeared, and blue and gold smoke went into the ground.

When the king saw the fish, he said to the fisherman, 'Those are beautiful fish! I will give you gold for them.' Then he said to his servant, 'Take these fish to the cook. We will eat them today.'

◆

The fisherman took his gold home to his family. They ate a wonderful dinner of bread, meat, fruit, vegetables and *no* fish. For the first time in their lives, they were not hungry.

The king's cook put the fish over the fire. They started to cook. Suddenly, the smoke from the fire went blue and gold and a strange woman appeared in the kitchen. She spoke to the fish.

'Fish, fish! Are you doing your work?' The fish did not answer. Then their heads went up, and they said, 'We are, and we are happy.' The strange woman pushed the fish into the fire. The smoke from the fire went blue and gold and the woman disappeared into it.

The king and his servant came into the kitchen. 'I am waiting for the fish. Where are they?' he said to the cook. He saw that the fish were in the fire and he could not eat them. The cook told him about the strange woman. The king wanted to see the woman so he sent for the fisherman. 'Bring me three more fish!' he said.

When the fisherman came back with three more fish, the king gave him more gold. The cook put the fish over the fire. This time the smoke from the fire went red and gold and a big man with red hair appeared.

'Fish, fish! Are you doing your work?' The fish answered, 'We are, we are! And we are happy!' And the same thing happened. The man pushed the fish into the fire and disappeared into the red and gold smoke.

The king did not speak for a minute. This was magic! Then he turned to the fisherman. 'Where do you get these fish?' he asked.

'I get them from a sea of blue and gold water over the mountain.'

'Do *you* know this sea?' the king asked his servant.

'No. I often go across the mountain, but there is no blue and gold sea.'

'Will you take us there?' the king asked the fisherman.

◆

The king and his men followed the fisherman over the mountain to the sea of blue and gold and there they saw the wonderful fish. The fish were jewels in the water.

'Wait here,' said the king. He took two men and went round the sea. There they came to a great house of red stone. All round the house were gardens of wonderful flowers. There was no answer at the door. But it was open so the king went in. He saw many beautiful rooms but no people. He came into a very large room with high windows. Somebody spoke: 'When will I die? I don't want to live.'

The king saw a young man at the other end of the room. He was on the floor with a coat over his feet.

'I know you are a king,' said the young man, 'but I cannot stand up.' The king took away the coat and saw that his feet were fine white stone.

'What is this?' cried the king. 'Why do you have stone feet? Why do the fish talk? Why does a man with red hair appear from nowhere in my kitchen? What is happening? Tell me.'

'I will tell you,' said the young man. 'Please sit down and listen. There was once a great city in this place. My father was king of that city, and I was a prince. Then my father died and I was the king. I married a beautiful woman. She was my queen but she did not love me. She loved a servant. When I learnt about him, I wanted to kill that servant. We had a fight. I hurt him but I didn't kill him. He could not use his legs.

'My wife was very angry. She can do magic and she changed my feet to white stone. Then *I* could not use *my* legs. That was not the end of it. Three mountains and a blue and gold sea appeared in place of the city. She changed the men and women of the city into fish.

'There is a little house of white stone in the garden of this house. The servant lives there. He cannot walk. My wife visits him every day.'

◆

The king went into the garden and thought for some time. Then he went to the house of white stone. He found the servant inside and killed him. He put the servant under the bed and then climbed onto it. He pulled the servant's jacket over his face. Some time later, the queen came in.

'Are you happy, my dearest servant?' she asked.

'No,' said the king. 'I cannot sleep. Somebody is crying. The young king is crying because of his stone feet.'

The queen went to the young king and threw some magic water over his feet. He stood up and walked.

Then she came back to the house of white stone. 'And I cannot sleep,' the king said,' because the men and women of the city cry at night. They do not want to be fish.'

So the queen went to the blue and gold sea. She said some magic words. A great city appeared all round her. Men and women ran happily through the streets and in and out of the houses. Then the queen came back to the house of white stone.

'Are you happy now, my dear servant?' she asked.

'Yes, my love,' he said. 'Come near me.' She came near him. 'Come nearer. I want to put my arms round you.' She came nearer his bed. He put his arms round her. In one hand he had a knife, and he killed her.

He went back to the young king. 'Your queen is dead. The city and its people are living.'

The older king and the young king were friends after that. One city helped the other city. But nobody ate fish again.

The fisherman and his family were happy. The two kings sent them gold and beautiful things. They were never hungry again.

The White Birds

Once there was a king with ten sons and one daughter. Their mother died when the daughter, Elisa, was born. They were very good, happy children.

Then the king fell in love with another woman and he married her. He loved his new queen and in his eyes she was always right. But she was a bad, jealous woman. She hated the king's ten sons, and she wanted to send them away. Love made the king stupid. It can make everybody stupid.

The poor old king sadly said goodbye to his sons. Then the queen took them outside the city walls. She said some magic words and changed the ten boys into ten white birds.

'Fly away to another country,' she said. 'Make your homes in treetops. Find your food on the ground.'

And the ten brothers flew high into the sky and away over mountains and rivers. They came to a great sea and they made their home in some trees next to it.

◆

When Elisa learned about her brothers, she ran away from the king's house. She cried for hours. She walked for days. She did not use her eyes – she followed her love for her brothers. 'One day I will find them,' she thought. And her love took her near their home by the great sea.

Night came and Elisa fell asleep under a tree. All night the fairies watched her and no dangerous animal came near her. The next morning she walked again. She met an old woman.

'What are you doing here? Can't a brother or friend help you?' asked the old woman. She gave Elisa some good food.

Elisa told her the story of her brothers. 'I am looking for ten fine princes on ten white horses,' she said. 'Do you know of them?'

'Ten princes?' said the woman. 'No, but I saw ten white birds this morning. They had gold feet and jewels for eyes. Perhaps they were princes. They were by the river.'

She took Elisa to the river. Elisa followed the river to the great sea. She saw ten fine white birds. Their gold feet and jewel-eyes shone in the sun. All round her Elisa saw pretty flowers and beautiful trees.

Elisa built a small house from sticks. She found flowers and put them round the walls. When she came back, she found bread, eggs and fish near the door.

That night her brothers came to her. She cried. 'Don't be sad,' they said. 'We'll tell you some stories.' Their stories were funny and after a time she smiled. Then she laughed.

When it was late, the brothers flew up into a tree. 'Sleep well, Elisa,' they said. 'We are watching you.'

In her sleep, Elisa saw the old woman again. Now she was a beautiful fairy.

'Do you want to help your brothers?' she asked.

'Yes!' cried Elisa. 'Of course!'

'Are you strong?'

'Yes! I am strong.'

'Then listen to my words and follow them. There are gold flowers near your little house. Take some home and put them in water from the river. Wash them many times and then make them into coats. Ten coats of gold flowers, one for each brother.

'But remember these things: First, only *you* can make the coats. Second, you can only speak after you finish them. Don't speak before that, or your brothers will die. Can you do these things?'

'Yes,' answered the princess in her sleep, and she woke up. She looked outside her door and saw the gold flowers. She followed the fairy's words and she worked all day. When the sun went down, her fingers hurt. Her brothers came that night, but she did not speak to them.

'Why are you not speaking?' they asked. 'Is this the work of a bad fairy?' She showed them her work. She made a picture of ten coats on the ground with her finger. Then they understood – her work was for them. She worked and worked. Her brothers watched her.

◆

After two or three weeks, six coats were ready. Then one day, when she was by the river, a dog suddenly appeared. It jumped at her. Then other dogs came. They made a great noise and ran round her. A man came through the trees on a fine white horse, with many men behind him. Elisa looked at this man and she loved him.

'Who are you?' he asked her. 'Nobody lives here. Where are you from?' Elisa could not answer him. 'I am the king of a great country behind those mountains,' he told her. 'I often come here with my dogs and horses.'

He came every day and spoke to Elisa. They walked by the river and he told her about his life. He loved her and he wanted her to be his queen. But why did she not speak? She only spoke to him with her eyes.

In the end, he asked her, 'Will you be my queen?' Poor Elisa started to cry. She ran to the gold flowers.

'We will take the gold flowers and your work to my house. You can work there. Will you come?' She could not say no, because she loved him.

So Elisa and the king took the flowers and the coats – there were eight now – to his country. Her brothers were sad, but each day they flew high above the king's house.

◆

The king had a jealous younger brother. He wanted to be king and he wanted his brother to die. When the king married, he was angry. 'Now the king will have a son,' he thought, 'and I will never be king.' The king could not see inside his jealous brother's head. Because *he* was good and kind, everybody was good and kind.

One day the king had to leave the city for many days. He had to visit an important king in another country. The queen stayed at home and worked on her coats. Now she had nine. But she had no more flowers. She looked everywhere for the gold flowers. Then she found some flowers in a bad place. The people of the city threw their dead animals there.

'I cannot go there in daylight,' thought the queen. 'People will see me. They will not understand and I cannot tell them.' So she waited for night. Then she went out and got some flowers.

The king's younger brother saw the queen that night. He followed her and watched her. He waited the next night and followed her again. 'Now I have a plan,' he thought. He followed her for five nights. The next night he called the great men and women of the city to a place outside the city walls.

'Why are we meeting in the dark?' they asked.

So Elisa and the king took the flowers and the coats to his country.

'You will see,' he answered. 'You will learn something about your queen. Now, everybody, be quiet. Wait here with me and watch. What does our lovely queen do every night when the king is away? What do you think?'

A little time later, the queen appeared and got the flowers. She started to walk home, but the king's brother ran after her. He caught her arm. 'See!' he cried to the people. 'She is a bad woman. Only a bad woman looks for flowers in this place at night. She uses them for bad magic. She plans to kill our dear king, my brother. Why do you think she never speaks? Because she can only say magic words!'

People shouted, 'Kill her!', 'Put her on a fire!' And the king's brother said, 'Let's kill her before the king comes back. Or *she* will kill *him*!' He took the queen back to her room.

'Tomorrow,' he said to her before he closed the door, 'you will die!'

◆

The king and his servants were one day's journey away from the city. They found a place for the night and got off their horses. The king looked up and saw a white bird in the sky. The bird flew down to the king and the king's horse was afraid. The king shouted at the bird, but it did not go away.

Then he looked again and saw its gold feet and jewel-eyes. 'It is one of the fairy birds,' he thought. 'One of the queen's birds. She can understand their cries but I cannot. I think it wants me to go back quickly to the city.'

The king called his men. 'We are not staying here tonight,' he told them. 'We are going to the city now. We have to go back to the queen. Get ready quickly. I am leaving now. Follow me!'

The king and his men followed the white bird all night. The bird called to them, 'Quick-ly. Quick-ly.' In the city, Elisa worked all night with her gold flowers.

◆

The next morning the people of the city met in the big square in front of the king's house. They looked up at the sky. 'What are those white birds up there? Why are they making this noise?'

Men brought sticks and built a large fire. The birds flew down and round the men's heads. They took some sticks and flew away. But they could not take every stick.

The king's brother went to the queen's room. He brought her outside and into the square. She carried the gold coats in her arms, and the birds flew with her.

At the same time the king arrived at the opposite end of the square. His white bird flew over the people's heads.

'It is the queen,' cried the king. He fought his way through the people to the middle of the square.

'A fire?' cried the king. 'Why are you building a fire?' He looked at his younger brother and he knew! He was very angry, and the people were sorry. The younger brother turned to the people and shouted, 'Do we want her to die?' But the people did not answer 'yes'. They looked at their feet. Then a little boy at the front shouted, 'No.' And everybody shouted, 'No!'

The queen called to the white birds, 'Come here, my brothers.' The birds flew down to her feet. She threw her wonderful gold coats over them and they changed into ten fine young princes. The princes took the king's brother on top of the city walls and threw him to the ground. Boys ran after them and threw stones at him. Nobody saw him again.

The king put his arms round his queen. 'Speak to me now, my beautiful wife.'

◆

When you see white birds above you, listen. You will hear them cry, 'Quick-ly! Quick-ly'. Now you understand.

ACTIVITIES

The Table, the Donkey and the Stick and **The Prince and his Servants**

Before you read

1 Read the Introduction to the stories. Who . . .

    a was often ill but was a happy person?

    b got some new trousers for his story?

    c enjoyed the *Arabian Nights* when he was a child?

    d hated women?

    e told a new story every night for 1,001 nights?

2 Find the words in *italics* in your dictionary. They are all in the stories.

    a What is a *fairy*? And what is a *fairy tale*?

    b Read the sentences about *fairy tales*. Put these words in the right places.

       appear   jealous   magic   once

       Fairy tales are stories about strange worlds. Things happen by .....
       Strange people and things ..... from nowhere. People are often
       ..... of other people – they want their houses or jobs or wives.
       Fairy tales often start with these words: '..... there was a princess.'

    c Number these people 1 to 6. Number 1 is the most important in fairy tales.

       servant   poor man   princess   king   prince   queen

    d Which thing (on the right) is:

       brown or grey, with big ears?   *jewel*

       short, brown and hard?   *ice*

       hard, cold and wet?   *donkey*

       hard, cold and yellow?   *gold*

       hard, cold and different colours?   *stick*

After you read

3 Which words and sentences go with each person? Take one from each box.

    a Tom   donkey   'Out of the box.'   gold

    b Bob   stick   'I am hungry.'   food

    c Jack   table   'Bricklebat.'   help

4 Work with a friend. One of you is Tom, one is Tom's mother. Tom comes home with his magic table. Tom's mother invites everybody from the village for lunch. Have a conversation after lunch.

5 Answer these questions.

    a Why didn't the queen want her daughter to marry?

    b Why didn't the king want Prince Charles to go?

    c What three things does Prince Charles have to do for the queen?

    d How do these servants help Prince Charles?

        Fat Man Big Ear Long Arms Quick Eyes Cold Man

    e You are Prince Charles. You can only have two servants. Which servants will you have? Why?

    f Think of a sixth servant – a man or woman – for Prince Charles. What can they do? How can they help him?

The Glass Box

Before you read

6 This story is about a poor man, a magic box and a princess. What do you think will happen?

7 Find the word *stone* in your dictionary. What can you do with *stones*?

After you read

8 Finish these sentences:

    a The first dog's eyes are as large as . . . .

    b The second dog's eyes are as large as . . . .

    c The third dog's eyes are as big as . . . .

    There are two bigger dogs (not really!). What are their eyes as big as?

9 The king wants to find Hans's house. How does Anna help him? Which way is better?

10 Do you think Hans is a good man? What good thing does he do? What bad thing does he do?

The Fisherman and the Giant and **The White Birds**

Before you read

11 Look at the picture on page 24. Find these three things in the picture. Use your dictionary.

fisherman   giant   jar

12 The ten white birds in the second story are not really birds. What do you think they are?

After you read

13 Strange things happen in 'The Fisherman and the Giant'. Write down four strange things. Why do they happen?

14 Answer these questions about 'The White Birds'.

    a Why is the old king sad when he says goodbye to his sons?

    b How does Elisa find her brothers?

    c What does Elisa have to do before her brothers change back into princes again?

    d Why does Elisa cry when the king wants to marry her?

    e The king's younger brother sees Elisa at night, and makes a plan. What is his plan?

    f Why does the king follow the white bird all night? Why doesn't he wait for the morning?

15 We don't hear anything about Elisa's father and his second wife at the end of the story. What do you think happens to them?

Writing

16 Write Tom's or Bob's letter to his brother Jack in 'The Table, the Donkey and the Stick'. Start like this:

Dear Jack,

I am going to tell you a sad story.

17 Write about a picture in this book. Who are the people? What are they doing? What is happening?

18 Think of a fairy tale from your country. Tell the story.

19 Write a story. Use these words:

giant   gold   fire   bird   sea   jar   princess   cat   rain   thirsty   magic